Self-Care
Journal

Healthcare Workers
Edition

This journal is dedicated to all the healthcare workers who on some days feel like they have nothing left to give. You are not alone. Empathy is not infinite. Caring for others is more like a marathon than a sprint and establishing longevity in these careers involves a fundamental shift in mindset. Since you are witnessing the suffering of others frequently, it is imperative that you take care of your own mental well- being. This guided journal is a good first step in making self-care a habit by practising gratitude and building mental resilience daily.

The different prompts.

Self Care: What is one thing that you did during the day that actively helped your mental well-being? Examples include: exercising, meditation, preparing a healthy meal, engaging in a hobby, spending time with a friend.

Setting Boundaries: Did you notice yourself get overly invested and consciously set a boundary? When you notice that your stress levels are rising its okay to take a moment and step back (either mentally or even physically). Make sure to document this.

Gratitude
What are 3 things that you are grateful for today? Did a patient remind you why you chose this career? Did a coworker actively make your life a little easier? Chase the good in this section. Yes suffering exists and you will frequently witness it, but there is always good to be found.

Empathy Scale
After taking the time to reflect and practise gratitude, on a scale of 1-10 how much compassion do you have to give today. If it's only a 1 that's okay. This metric is just used to track trends & to be more aware of what we have to offer on a daily basis so we do not attempt to over-extend ourselves.

If you notice that you frequently have nothing left to give, there is no shame in asking for help.

My Mantra

Compassion fatigue does not make me weak. It is a sign that I have cared too much for too long. Today I begin to prioritize myself and my mental well-being, knowing that by doing so, I will be better prepared to care for those around me.

My why's

Why did you pick your career? Why do you continue to do this work? (It's okay for these to change over time)

_____
_____
_____
_____
_____
_____
_____
_____
_____
_____

Even on the darkest days, these why's will guide me.

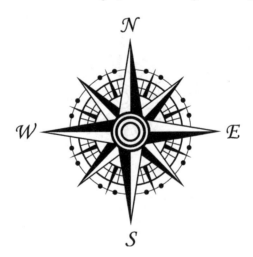

Date: ___/____/_____   **Empathy Scale:**

Self-Care:

_____

_____

_____

Boundaries

_____

_____

_____

Gratitude

_____

_____

_____

_____

Date: ___/____/_____   **Empathy Scale:**

Self-Care:

_____

_____

_____

Boundaries

_____

_____

Gratitude

_____

_____

_____

Date: ___/___/_____   **Empathy Scale:**

Self-Care:

_____

_____

_____

Boundaries

_____

_____

_____

Gratitude

_____

_____

_____

_____

Date: ___/___/_____   **Empathy Scale:**

Self-Care:

_____

_____

_____

Boundaries

_____

_____

_____

Gratitude

_____

_____

_____

_____

Date: ___/___/_____   **Empathy Scale:**

Self-Care:

_____

_____

_____

Boundaries

_____

_____

_____

Gratitude

_____

_____

_____

_____

Date: ___/___/_____   **Empathy Scale:**

Self-Care:

_____

_____

_____

Boundaries

_____

_____

_____

Gratitude

_____

_____

_____

_____

Date: ___/____/_____   **Empathy Scale:**

Self-Care:

_____

_____

_____

Boundaries

_____

_____

_____

Gratitude

_____

_____

_____

_____

Date: ___/____/_____   **Empathy Scale:**

Self-Care:

_____

_____

_____

Boundaries

_____

_____

_____

Gratitude

_____

_____

_____

_____

Date: ___/_____/_____   **Empathy Scale:**

Self-Care:

_____

_____

_____

Boundaries

_____

_____

_____

Gratitude

_____

_____

_____

_____

Date: ___/_____/_____   **Empathy Scale:**

Self-Care:

_____

_____

_____

Boundaries

_____

_____

_____

Gratitude

_____

_____

_____

Date: ___/____/_____   **Empathy Scale:**

Self-Care:

_____

_____

_____

Boundaries

_____

_____

_____

Gratitude

_____

_____

_____

_____

Date: ___/____/_____   **Empathy Scale:**

Self-Care:

_____

_____

_____

Boundaries

_____

_____

_____

Gratitude

_____

_____

_____

_____

Date: ___/___/_____   **Empathy Scale:**

Self-Care:

_____

_____

_____

Boundaries

_____

_____

Gratitude

_____

_____

_____

_____

Date: ___/___/_____   **Empathy Scale:**

Self-Care:

_____

_____

_____

Boundaries

_____

_____

Gratitude

_____

_____

_____

Date: ___/___/_____   **Empathy Scale:**

Self-Care:

_____

_____

_____

Boundaries

_____

_____

_____

Gratitude

_____

_____

_____

_____

Date: ___/___/_____   **Empathy Scale:**

Self-Care:

_____

_____

_____

Boundaries

_____

_____

_____

Gratitude

_____

_____

_____

_____

Date: ___/___/_____   **Empathy Scale:**

Self-Care:

_____

_____

_____

Boundaries

_____

_____

_____

Gratitude

_____

_____

_____

_____

Date: ___/___/_____   **Empathy Scale:**

Self-Care:

_____

_____

_____

Boundaries

_____

_____

_____

Gratitude

_____

_____

_____

_____

Date: ___/____/_____   **Empathy Scale:**

Self-Care:

_____

_____

_____

Boundaries

_____

_____

_____

Gratitude

_____

_____

_____

_____

Date: ___/____/_____   **Empathy Scale:**

Self-Care:

_____

_____

_____

Boundaries

_____

_____

_____

Gratitude

_____

_____

_____

_____

Date: ___/___/_____   **Empathy Scale:**

Self-Care:

_____

_____

_____

Boundaries

_____

_____

_____

Gratitude

_____

_____

_____

_____

Date: ___/___/_____   **Empathy Scale:**

Self-Care:

_____

_____

_____

Boundaries

_____

_____

_____

Gratitude

_____

_____

_____

_____

Date: ___/_____/_____   **Empathy Scale:**

Self-Care:

_____

_____

_____

Boundaries

_____

_____

_____

Gratitude

_____

_____

_____

_____

Date: ___/_____/_____   **Empathy Scale:**

Self-Care:

_____

_____

_____

Boundaries

_____

_____

_____

Gratitude

_____

_____

_____

_____

Date: ___/____/_____   **Empathy Scale:**

Self-Care:

_____

_____

_____

Boundaries

_____

_____

_____

Gratitude

_____

_____

_____

_____

Date: ___/____/_____   **Empathy Scale:**

Self-Care:

_____

_____

_____

Boundaries

_____

_____

_____

Gratitude

_____

_____

_____

_____

Date: ___/___/_____   **Empathy Scale:**

Self-Care:

_____

_____

_____

Boundaries

_____

_____

_____

Gratitude

_____

_____

_____

_____

Date: ___/___/_____   **Empathy Scale:**

Self-Care:

_____

_____

_____

Boundaries

_____

_____

_____

Gratitude

_____

_____

_____

_____

Date: ___/___/_____   **Empathy Scale:**

Self-Care:

_____

_____

_____

Boundaries

_____

_____

_____

Gratitude

_____

_____

_____

_____

Date: ___/___/_____   **Empathy Scale:**

Self-Care:

_____

_____

_____

Boundaries

_____

_____

_____

Gratitude

_____

_____

_____

_____

Date: ___/____/_____   **Empathy Scale:**

Self-Care:

_____

_____

_____

Boundaries

_____

_____

_____

Gratitude

_____

_____

_____

_____

Date: ___/____/_____   **Empathy Scale:**

Self-Care:

_____

_____

_____

Boundaries

_____

_____

Gratitude

_____

_____

_____

_____

Date: ___/____/_____   **Empathy Scale:**

Self-Care:

_____

_____

_____

Boundaries

_____

_____

_____

Gratitude

_____

_____

_____

_____

Date: ___/____/_____   **Empathy Scale:**

Self-Care:

_____

_____

_____

Boundaries

_____

_____

_____

Gratitude

_____

_____

_____

_____

Date: ___/____/_____   **Empathy Scale:**

Self-Care:

_____

_____

_____

Boundaries

_____

_____

Gratitude

_____

_____

_____

_____

Date: ___/____/_____   **Empathy Scale:**

Self-Care:

_____

_____

_____

Boundaries

_____

_____

Gratitude

_____

_____

_____

Date: ___/____/_____   **Empathy Scale:**

Self-Care:

_____

_____

_____

Boundaries

_____

_____

_____

Gratitude

_____

_____

_____

_____

Date: ___/____/_____   **Empathy Scale:**

Self-Care:

_____

_____

_____

Boundaries

_____

_____

_____

Gratitude

_____

_____

_____

Date: ___/___/_____   **Empathy Scale:**

Self-Care:

_____

_____

_____

Boundaries

_____

_____

_____

Gratitude

_____

_____

_____

_____

Date: ___/___/_____   **Empathy Scale:**

Self-Care:

_____

_____

_____

Boundaries

_____

_____

Gratitude

_____

_____

_____

Date: ___/____/_____   **Empathy Scale:**

Self-Care:

_____

_____

_____

Boundaries

_____

_____

_____

Gratitude

_____

_____

_____

Date: ___/____/_____   **Empathy Scale:**

Self-Care:

_____

_____

_____

Boundaries

_____

_____

_____

Gratitude

_____

_____

_____

Date: ___/____/_____   **Empathy Scale:**

Self-Care:

_____

_____

_____

Boundaries

_____

_____

_____

Gratitude

_____

_____

_____

_____

Date: ___/____/_____   **Empathy Scale:**

Self-Care:

_____

_____

_____

Boundaries

_____

_____

Gratitude

_____

_____

_____

_____

Date: ___/____/_____   **Empathy Scale:**

Self-Care:

_____

_____

_____

Boundaries

_____

_____

_____

Gratitude

_____

_____

_____

_____

Date: ___/____/_____   **Empathy Scale:**

Self-Care:

_____

_____

_____

Boundaries

_____

_____

_____

Gratitude

_____

_____

_____

Date: ___/____/_____ **Empathy Scale:**

Self-Care:

_____

_____

_____

Boundaries

_____

_____

_____

Gratitude

_____

_____

_____

_____

Date: ___/____/_____ **Empathy Scale:**

Self-Care:

_____

_____

_____

Boundaries

_____

_____

Gratitude

_____

_____

_____

Date: ___/___/_____   **Empathy Scale:**

Self-Care:

_____

_____

_____

Boundaries

_____

_____

_____

Gratitude

_____

_____

_____

_____

Date: ___/___/_____   **Empathy Scale:**

Self-Care:

_____

_____

_____

Boundaries

_____

_____

_____

Gratitude

_____

_____

_____

_____

Date: ___/____/_____   **Empathy Scale:**

Self-Care:

_____

_____

_____

Boundaries

_____

_____

_____

Gratitude

_____

_____

_____

_____

Date: ___/____/_____   **Empathy Scale:**

Self-Care:

_____

_____

_____

Boundaries

_____

_____

_____

Gratitude

_____

_____

_____

_____

Date: ___/____/_____   **Empathy Scale:**

Self-Care:

_____

_____

_____

Boundaries

_____

_____

_____

Gratitude

_____

_____

_____

_____

Date: ___/____/_____   **Empathy Scale:**

Self-Care:

_____

_____

_____

Boundaries

_____

_____

_____

Gratitude

_____

_____

_____

Date: ___/____/_____   **Empathy Scale:**

Self-Care:

_____

_____

_____

Boundaries

_____

_____

_____

Gratitude

_____

_____

_____

_____

Date: ___/____/_____   **Empathy Scale:**

Self-Care:

_____

_____

_____

Boundaries

_____

_____

Gratitude

_____

_____

_____

Date: ___/___/_____   **Empathy Scale:**

Self-Care:

_____

_____

_____

Boundaries

_____

_____

_____

Gratitude

_____

_____

_____

Date: ___/___/_____   **Empathy Scale:**

Self-Care:

_____

_____

_____

Boundaries

_____

_____

Gratitude

_____

_____

_____

Date: ___ / ____ / _____   **Empathy Scale:**

Self-Care:

_____

_____

_____

Boundaries

_____

_____

_____

Gratitude

_____

_____

_____

_____

Date: ___ / ____ / _____   **Empathy Scale:**

Self-Care:

_____

_____

_____

Boundaries

_____

_____

Gratitude

_____

_____

_____

_____

Date: ___/___/_____   **Empathy Scale:**

Self-Care:

_____

_____

_____

Boundaries

_____

_____

_____

Gratitude

_____

_____

_____

_____

Date: ___/___/_____   **Empathy Scale:**

Self-Care:

_____

_____

_____

Boundaries

_____

_____

_____

Gratitude

_____

_____

_____

_____

Date: ___/___/_____   **Empathy Scale:**

Self-Care:

_____

_____

_____

Boundaries

_____

_____

Gratitude

_____

_____

_____

_____

Date: ___/___/_____   **Empathy Scale:**

Self-Care:

_____

_____

_____

Boundaries

_____

_____

_____

Gratitude

_____

_____

_____

_____

Date: ___/____/_____   **Empathy Scale:**

Self-Care:

_____

_____

_____

Boundaries

_____

_____

_____

Gratitude

_____

_____

_____

_____

Date: ___/____/_____   **Empathy Scale:**

Self-Care:

_____

_____

_____

Boundaries

_____

_____

_____

Gratitude

_____

_____

_____

Date: ___/____/_____   **Empathy Scale:**

Self-Care:

_____

_____

_____

Boundaries

_____

_____

_____

Gratitude

_____

_____

_____

_____

Date: ___/____/_____   **Empathy Scale:**

Self-Care:

_____

_____

_____

Boundaries

_____

_____

Gratitude

_____

_____

_____

_____

Date: ___/___/_____   **Empathy Scale:**

Self-Care:

_____

_____

_____

Boundaries

_____

_____

_____

Gratitude

_____

_____

_____

_____

Date: ___/___/_____   **Empathy Scale:**

Self-Care:

_____

_____

_____

Boundaries

_____

_____

_____

Gratitude

_____

_____

_____

_____

Date: ___/___/_____   **Empathy Scale:**

Self-Care:

_____

_____

_____

Boundaries

_____

_____

_____

Gratitude

_____

_____

_____

_____

Date: ___/___/_____   **Empathy Scale:**

Self-Care:

_____

_____

_____

Boundaries

_____

_____

_____

Gratitude

_____

_____

_____

_____

Date: ___/____/_____   **Empathy Scale:**

Self-Care:

_____

_____

_____

Boundaries

_____

_____

_____

Gratitude

_____

_____

_____

_____

Date: ___/____/_____   **Empathy Scale:**

Self-Care:

_____

_____

_____

Boundaries

_____

_____

_____

Gratitude

_____

_____

_____

_____

Date: ___/____/_____   **Empathy Scale:**

Self-Care:

_____

_____

_____

Boundaries

_____

_____

_____

Gratitude

_____

_____

_____

_____

Date: ___/____/_____   **Empathy Scale:**

Self-Care:

_____

_____

_____

Boundaries

_____

_____

_____

Gratitude

_____

_____

_____

Date: ___/____/_____   **Empathy Scale:**

Self-Care:

_____

_____

_____

Boundaries

_____

_____

_____

Gratitude

_____

_____

_____

_____

Date: ___/____/_____   **Empathy Scale:**

Self-Care:

_____

_____

_____

Boundaries

_____

_____

Gratitude

_____

_____

_____

Date: ___/___/_____   **Empathy Scale:**

Self-Care:

_____

_____

_____

Boundaries

_____

_____

_____

Gratitude

_____

_____

_____

_____

Date: ___/___/_____   **Empathy Scale:**

Self-Care:

_____

_____

_____

Boundaries

_____

_____

_____

Gratitude

_____

_____

_____

Date: ___/____/_____   **Empathy Scale:**

Self-Care:

_____

_____

_____

Boundaries

_____

_____

_____

Gratitude

_____

_____

_____

_____

Date: ___/____/_____   **Empathy Scale:**

Self-Care:

_____

_____

_____

Boundaries

_____

_____

_____

Gratitude

_____

_____

_____

_____

Date: ___/___/_____   **Empathy Scale:**

Self-Care:

_____

_____

_____

Boundaries

_____

_____

_____

Gratitude

_____

_____

_____

_____

Date: ___/___/_____   **Empathy Scale:**

Self-Care:

_____

_____

_____

Boundaries

_____

_____

_____

Gratitude

_____

_____

_____

_____

Date: ___/_____/_____   **Empathy Scale:**

Self-Care:

_____

_____

_____

Boundaries

_____

_____

_____

Gratitude

_____

_____

_____

_____

Date: ___/_____/_____   **Empathy Scale:**

Self-Care:

_____

_____

_____

Boundaries

_____

_____

_____

Gratitude

_____

_____

_____

_____

Date: ___/____/_____   **Empathy Scale:**

Self-Care:

_____

_____

_____

Boundaries

_____

_____

_____

Gratitude

_____

_____

_____

_____

Date: ___/____/_____   **Empathy Scale:**

Self-Care:

_____

_____

_____

Boundaries

_____

_____

Gratitude

_____

_____

_____

Date: ___/____/_____   **Empathy Scale:**

Self-Care:

_____

_____

_____

Boundaries

_____

_____

_____

Gratitude

_____

_____

_____

_____

Date: ___/____/_____   **Empathy Scale:**

Self-Care:

_____

_____

_____

Boundaries

_____

_____

_____

Gratitude

_____

_____

_____

_____

Date: ___/___/_____   **Empathy Scale:**

Self-Care:

_____

_____

_____

Boundaries

_____

_____

Gratitude

_____

_____

_____

_____

Date: ___/___/_____   **Empathy Scale:**

Self-Care:

_____

_____

_____

Boundaries

_____

_____

Gratitude

_____

_____

_____

Date: ___/____/_____   **Empathy Scale:**

Self-Care:

_____

_____

_____

Boundaries

_____

_____

_____

Gratitude

_____

_____

_____

_____

Date: ___/____/_____   **Empathy Scale:**

Self-Care:

_____

_____

_____

Boundaries

_____

_____

_____

Gratitude

_____

_____

_____

_____

Date: ___/____/_____   **Empathy Scale:**

Self-Care:

_____

_____

_____

Boundaries

_____

_____

_____

Gratitude

_____

_____

_____

_____

Date: ___/____/_____   **Empathy Scale:**

Self-Care:

_____

_____

_____

Boundaries

_____

_____

_____

Gratitude

_____

_____

_____

_____

Date: ___/_____/_____   **Empathy Scale:**

Self-Care:

_____

_____

_____

Boundaries

_____

_____

_____

Gratitude

_____

_____

_____

_____

Date: ___/_____/_____   **Empathy Scale:**

Self-Care:

_____

_____

_____

Boundaries

_____

_____

_____

Gratitude

_____

_____

_____

_____

Date: ___/____/_____   **Empathy Scale:**

Self-Care:

_____

_____

_____

Boundaries

_____

_____

_____

Gratitude

_____

_____

_____

_____

Date: ___/____/_____   **Empathy Scale:**

Self-Care:

_____

_____

_____

Boundaries

_____

_____

_____

Gratitude

_____

_____

_____

_____

Date: ___/____/_____   **Empathy Scale:**

Self-Care:

_____

_____

_____

Boundaries

_____

_____

_____

Gratitude

_____

_____

_____

_____

Date: ___/____/_____   **Empathy Scale:**

Self-Care:

_____

_____

_____

Boundaries

_____

_____

_____

Gratitude

_____

_____

_____

Date: ___/____/_____   **Empathy Scale:**

Self-Care:

_____

_____

_____

Boundaries

_____

_____

_____

Gratitude

_____

_____

_____

_____

Date: ___/____/_____   **Empathy Scale:**

Self-Care:

_____

_____

_____

Boundaries

_____

_____

Gratitude

_____

_____

_____

Date: ___/____/_____   **Empathy Scale:**

Self-Care:

_____

_____

_____

Boundaries

_____

_____

_____

Gratitude

_____

_____

_____

_____

Date: ___/____/_____   **Empathy Scale:**

Self-Care:

_____

_____

_____

Boundaries

_____

_____

_____

Gratitude

_____

_____

_____

_____

Date: ___/____/_____   **Empathy Scale:**

Self-Care:

_____

_____

_____

Boundaries

_____

_____

Gratitude

_____

_____

_____

_____

Date: ___/____/_____   **Empathy Scale:**

Self-Care:

_____

_____

_____

Boundaries

_____

_____

_____

Gratitude

_____

_____

_____

Date: ___/____/_____   **Empathy Scale:**

Self-Care:

_____

_____

_____

Boundaries

_____

_____

_____

Gratitude

_____

_____

_____

_____

Date: ___/____/_____   **Empathy Scale:**

Self-Care:

_____

_____

_____

Boundaries

_____

_____

_____

Gratitude

_____

_____

_____

_____

Date: ___/____/_____   **Empathy Scale:**

Self-Care:

_____

_____

_____

Boundaries

_____

_____

_____

Gratitude

_____

_____

_____

_____

Date: ___/____/_____   **Empathy Scale:**

Self-Care:

_____

_____

_____

Boundaries

_____

_____

_____

Gratitude

_____

_____

_____

_____

Date: ___/___/_____   **Empathy Scale:**

Self-Care:

_____

_____

_____

Boundaries

_____

_____

_____

Gratitude

_____

_____

_____

_____

Date: ___/___/_____   **Empathy Scale:**

Self-Care:

_____

_____

_____

Boundaries

_____

_____

_____

Gratitude

_____

_____

_____

_____

Date: ___/____/_____   **Empathy Scale:**

Self-Care:

_____

_____

_____

Boundaries

_____

_____

_____

Gratitude

_____

_____

_____

_____

Date: ___/____/_____   **Empathy Scale:**

Self-Care:

_____

_____

_____

Boundaries

_____

_____

_____

Gratitude

_____

_____

_____

_____

Date: ___/____/_____   **Empathy Scale:**

Self-Care:

_____

_____

_____

Boundaries

_____

_____

_____

Gratitude

_____

_____

_____

_____

Date: ___/____/_____   **Empathy Scale:**

Self-Care:

_____

_____

_____

Boundaries

_____

_____

_____

Gratitude

_____

_____

_____

Date: ___/___/_____   **Empathy Scale:**

Self-Care:

_____

_____

_____

Boundaries

_____

_____

_____

Gratitude

_____

_____

_____

_____

Date: ___/___/_____   **Empathy Scale:**

Self-Care:

_____

_____

_____

Boundaries

_____

_____

_____

Gratitude

_____

_____

_____

_____

Date: ___/___/_____   **Empathy Scale:**

Self-Care:

_____

_____

_____

Boundaries

_____

_____

_____

Gratitude

_____

_____

_____

_____

Date: ___/___/_____   **Empathy Scale:**

Self-Care:

_____

_____

_____

Boundaries

_____

_____

_____

Gratitude

_____

_____

_____

_____

Date: ___/___/_____　　　　**Empathy Scale:**

Self-Care:

_____

_____

_____

Boundaries

_____

_____

_____

Gratitude

_____

_____

_____

_____

Date: ___/___/_____　　　　**Empathy Scale:**

Self-Care:

_____

_____

_____

Boundaries

_____

_____

Gratitude

_____

_____

_____

Date: ___/____/_____   **Empathy Scale:**

Self-Care:

_____

_____

_____

Boundaries

_____

_____

_____

Gratitude

_____

_____

_____

_____

Date: ___/____/_____   **Empathy Scale:**

Self-Care:

_____

_____

_____

Boundaries

_____

_____

_____

Gratitude

_____

_____

_____

_____

Date: ___/____/_____   **Empathy Scale:**

Self-Care:

_____

_____

_____

Boundaries

_____

_____

_____

Gratitude

_____

_____

_____

_____

Date: ___/____/_____   **Empathy Scale:**

Self-Care:

_____

_____

_____

Boundaries

_____

_____

_____

Gratitude

_____

_____

_____

_____

Date: ___/___/_____   **Empathy Scale:**

Self-Care:

_____

_____

_____

Boundaries

_____

_____

_____

Gratitude

_____

_____

_____

_____

Date: ___/___/_____   **Empathy Scale:**

Self-Care:

_____

_____

_____

Boundaries

_____

_____

Gratitude

_____

_____

_____

Date: ___/____/_____   **Empathy Scale:**

Self-Care:

_____

_____

_____

Boundaries

_____

_____

_____

Gratitude

_____

_____

_____

_____

Date: ___/____/_____   **Empathy Scale:**

Self-Care:

_____

_____

_____

Boundaries

_____

_____

_____

Gratitude

_____

_____

_____

_____

Date: ___/____/_____   **Empathy Scale:**

Self-Care:

_____

_____

_____

Boundaries

_____

_____

_____

Gratitude

_____

_____

_____

_____

Date: ___/____/_____   **Empathy Scale:**

Self-Care:

_____

_____

_____

Boundaries

_____

_____

_____

Gratitude

_____

_____

_____

_____

Date: ___/___/_____   **Empathy Scale:**

Self-Care:

_____

_____

_____

Boundaries

_____

_____

_____

Gratitude

_____

_____

_____

_____

Date: ___/___/_____   **Empathy Scale:**

Self-Care:

_____

_____

_____

Boundaries

_____

_____

_____

Gratitude

_____

_____

_____

_____

Date: ___/____/_____   **Empathy Scale:**

Self-Care:

_____

_____

_____

Boundaries

_____

_____

_____

Gratitude

_____

_____

_____

_____

Date: ___/____/_____   **Empathy Scale:**

Self-Care:

_____

_____

_____

Boundaries

_____

_____

_____

Gratitude

_____

_____

_____

_____

Date: ___/____/_____   **Empathy Scale:**

Self-Care:

_____

_____

_____

Boundaries

_____

_____

_____

Gratitude

_____

_____

_____

_____

Date: ___/____/_____   **Empathy Scale:**

Self-Care:

_____

_____

Boundaries

_____

_____

Gratitude

_____

_____

_____

Date: ___/____/_____   **Empathy Scale:**

Self-Care:

_____

_____

_____

Boundaries

_____

_____

_____

Gratitude

_____

_____

_____

_____

Date: ___/____/_____   **Empathy Scale:**

Self-Care:

_____

_____

_____

Boundaries

_____

_____

_____

Gratitude

_____

_____

_____

Date: ___/___/_____　　　　　**Empathy Scale:**

Self-Care:

_____

_____

_____

Boundaries

_____

_____

_____

Gratitude

_____

_____

_____

_____

Date: ___/___/_____　　　　　**Empathy Scale:**

Self-Care:

_____

_____

_____

Boundaries

_____

_____

Gratitude

_____

_____

_____

Date: ___/____/_____   **Empathy Scale:**

Self-Care:

_____

_____

_____

Boundaries

_____

_____

_____

Gratitude

_____

_____

_____

_____

Date: ___/____/_____   **Empathy Scale:**

Self-Care:

_____

_____

_____

Boundaries

_____

_____

Gratitude

_____

_____

_____

Date: ___/_____/_____   **Empathy Scale:**

Self-Care:

_____

_____

_____

Boundaries

_____

_____

_____

Gratitude

_____

_____

_____

_____

Date: ___/_____/_____   **Empathy Scale:**

Self-Care:

_____

_____

_____

Boundaries

_____

_____

_____

Gratitude

_____

_____

_____

Date: ___/___/_____   **Empathy Scale:**

Self-Care:

_____

_____

_____

Boundaries

_____

_____

_____

Gratitude

_____

_____

_____

_____

Date: ___/___/_____   **Empathy Scale:**

Self-Care:

_____

_____

_____

Boundaries

_____

_____

_____

Gratitude

_____

_____

_____

Date: ___/____/_____   **Empathy Scale:**

Self-Care:

_____

_____

_____

Boundaries

_____

_____

_____

Gratitude

_____

_____

_____

_____

Date: ___/____/_____   **Empathy Scale:**

Self-Care:

_____

_____

_____

Boundaries

_____

_____

_____

Gratitude

_____

_____

_____

_____

Date: ___/____/_____   **Empathy Scale:**

Self-Care:

_____

_____

_____

Boundaries

_____

_____

_____

Gratitude

_____

_____

_____

_____

Date: ___/____/_____   **Empathy Scale:**

Self-Care:

_____

_____

_____

Boundaries

_____

_____

_____

Gratitude

_____

_____

_____

_____

Date: ___/___/_____   **Empathy Scale:**

Self-Care:

_____

_____

_____

Boundaries

_____

_____

_____

Gratitude

_____

_____

_____

_____

Date: ___/___/_____   **Empathy Scale:**

Self-Care:

_____

_____

_____

Boundaries

_____

_____

_____

Gratitude

_____

_____

_____

_____

Date: ___/___/_____   **Empathy Scale:**

Self-Care:

_____

_____

_____

Boundaries

_____

_____

_____

Gratitude

_____

_____

_____

_____

Date: ___/___/_____   **Empathy Scale:**

Self-Care:

_____

_____

_____

Boundaries

_____

_____

_____

Gratitude

_____

_____

_____

_____

Date: ___/____/_____   **Empathy Scale:**

Self-Care:

_____

_____

_____

Boundaries

_____

_____

_____

Gratitude

_____

_____

_____

_____

Date: ___/____/_____   **Empathy Scale:**

Self-Care:

_____

_____

_____

Boundaries

_____

_____

Gratitude

_____

_____

_____

_____

Date: ___/___/_____   **Empathy Scale:**

Self-Care:

_____

_____

_____

Boundaries

_____

_____

_____

Gratitude

_____

_____

_____

_____

Date: ___/___/_____   **Empathy Scale:**

Self-Care:

_____

_____

_____

Boundaries

_____

_____

_____

Gratitude

_____

_____

_____

_____

Date: ___/___/_____   **Empathy Scale:**

Self-Care:

_____

_____

_____

Boundaries

_____

_____

Gratitude

_____

_____

_____

_____

Date: ___/___/_____   **Empathy Scale:**

Self-Care:

_____

_____

_____

Boundaries

_____

_____

Gratitude

_____

_____

_____

Date: ___/____/_____   **Empathy Scale:**

Self-Care:

_____

_____

_____

Boundaries

_____

_____

_____

Gratitude

_____

_____

_____

_____

Date: ___/____/_____   **Empathy Scale:**

Self-Care:

_____

_____

_____

Boundaries

_____

_____

_____

Gratitude

_____

_____

_____

_____

Date: ___/___/_____   **Empathy Scale:**

Self-Care:

_____

_____

_____

Boundaries

_____

_____

_____

Gratitude

_____

_____

_____

_____

Date: ___/___/_____   **Empathy Scale:**

Self-Care:

_____

_____

_____

Boundaries

_____

_____

_____

Gratitude

_____

_____

_____

_____

Date: ___/___/_____   **Empathy Scale:**

Self-Care:

_____

_____

_____

Boundaries

_____

_____

_____

Gratitude

_____

_____

_____

_____

Date: ___/___/_____   **Empathy Scale:**

Self-Care:

_____

_____

_____

Boundaries

_____

_____

_____

Gratitude

_____

_____

_____

_____

Date: ___/___/_____   **Empathy Scale:**

Self-Care:

_____

_____

_____

Boundaries

_____

_____

_____

Gratitude

_____

_____

_____

_____

Date: ___/___/_____   **Empathy Scale:**

Self-Care:

_____

_____

_____

Boundaries

_____

_____

Gratitude

_____

_____

_____

_____

Date: ___/___/_____   **Empathy Scale:**

Self-Care:

_____

_____

_____

Boundaries

_____

_____

_____

Gratitude

_____

_____

_____

_____

Date: ___/___/_____   **Empathy Scale:**

Self-Care:

_____

_____

_____

Boundaries

_____

_____

_____

Gratitude

_____

_____

_____

_____

Date: ___/_____/_____   **Empathy Scale:**

Self-Care:

_____

_____

_____

Boundaries

_____

_____

_____

Gratitude

_____

_____

_____

_____

Date: ___/_____/_____   **Empathy Scale:**

Self-Care:

_____

_____

_____

Boundaries

_____

_____

Gratitude

_____

_____

_____

Date: ___/___/_____   **Empathy Scale:**

Self-Care:

_____

_____

_____

Boundaries

_____

_____

_____

Gratitude

_____

_____

_____

_____

Date: ___/___/_____   **Empathy Scale:**

Self-Care:

_____

_____

_____

Boundaries

_____

_____

_____

Gratitude

_____

_____

_____

_____

Date: ___/___/_____   **Empathy Scale:**

Self-Care:

_____

_____

_____

Boundaries

_____

_____

_____

Gratitude

_____

_____

_____

_____

Date: ___/___/_____   **Empathy Scale:**

Self-Care:

_____

_____

_____

Boundaries

_____

_____

Gratitude

_____

_____

_____

Date: ___/___/_____   **Empathy Scale:**

Self-Care:

_____

_____

_____

Boundaries

_____

_____

_____

Gratitude

_____

_____

_____

_____

Date: ___/___/_____   **Empathy Scale:**

Self-Care:

_____

_____

_____

Boundaries

_____

_____

_____

Gratitude

_____

_____

_____

Date: ___/____/_____   **Empathy Scale:**

Self-Care:

_____

_____

_____

Boundaries

_____

_____

_____

Gratitude

_____

_____

_____

_____

Date: ___/____/_____   **Empathy Scale:**

Self-Care:

_____

_____

_____

Boundaries

_____

_____

_____

Gratitude

_____

_____

_____

_____

Date: ___/_____/_____   **Empathy Scale:**

Self-Care:

_____

_____

_____

Boundaries

_____

_____

_____

Gratitude

_____

_____

_____

_____

Date: ___/_____/_____   **Empathy Scale:**

Self-Care:

_____

_____

_____

Boundaries

_____

_____

_____

Gratitude

_____

_____

_____

_____

Date: ___/_____/_____   **Empathy Scale:**

Self-Care:

_____

_____

_____

Boundaries

_____

_____

_____

Gratitude

_____

_____

_____

_____

Date: ___/_____/_____   **Empathy Scale:**

Self-Care:

_____

_____

_____

Boundaries

_____

_____

_____

Gratitude

_____

_____

_____

_____

Date: ___/____/_____   **Empathy Scale:**

Self-Care:

_____

_____

_____

Boundaries

_____

_____

_____

Gratitude

_____

_____

_____

_____

Date: ___/____/_____   **Empathy Scale:**

Self-Care:

_____

_____

_____

Boundaries

_____

_____

_____

Gratitude

_____

_____

_____

Date: ___/____/_____   **Empathy Scale:**

Self-Care:

_____

_____

_____

Boundaries

_____

_____

_____

Gratitude

_____

_____

_____

_____

Date: ___/____/_____   **Empathy Scale:**

Self-Care:

_____

_____

_____

Boundaries

_____

_____

_____

Gratitude

_____

_____

_____

_____

Date: ___/____/_____   **Empathy Scale:**

Self-Care:

_____

_____

_____

Boundaries

_____

_____

_____

Gratitude

_____

_____

_____

_____

Date: ___/____/_____   **Empathy Scale:**

Self-Care:

_____

_____

_____

Boundaries

_____

_____

_____

Gratitude

_____

_____

_____

_____

Date: ___/___/_____   **Empathy Scale:**

Self-Care:

_____

_____

_____

Boundaries

_____

_____

_____

Gratitude

_____

_____

_____

_____

Date: ___/___/_____   **Empathy Scale:**

Self-Care:

_____

_____

_____

Boundaries

_____

_____

_____

Gratitude

_____

_____

_____

_____

Date: ___ / ____ / _____   **Empathy Scale:**

Self-Care:

_____

_____

_____

Boundaries

_____

_____

_____

Gratitude

_____

_____

_____

_____

Date: ___ / ____ / _____   **Empathy Scale:**

Self-Care:

_____

_____

_____

Boundaries

_____

_____

_____

Gratitude

_____

_____

_____

_____

Date: ___/___/_____   **Empathy Scale:**

Self-Care:

_____

_____

_____

Boundaries

_____

_____

_____

Gratitude

_____

_____

_____

_____

Date: ___/___/_____   **Empathy Scale:**

Self-Care:

_____

_____

_____

Boundaries

_____

_____

Gratitude

_____

_____

_____

_____

Date: ___/___/_____   **Empathy Scale:**

Self-Care:

_____

_____

_____

Boundaries

_____

_____

_____

Gratitude

_____

_____

_____

_____

Date: ___/___/_____   **Empathy Scale:**

Self-Care:

_____

_____

_____

Boundaries

_____

_____

_____

Gratitude

_____

_____

_____

Date: ___/____/_____   **Empathy Scale:**

Self-Care:

_____

_____

_____

Boundaries

_____

_____

_____

Gratitude

_____

_____

_____

_____

Date: ___/____/_____   **Empathy Scale:**

Self-Care:

_____

_____

_____

Boundaries

_____

_____

_____

Gratitude

_____

_____

_____

_____

Date: ___/____/_____   **Empathy Scale:**

Self-Care:

_____

_____

_____

Boundaries

_____

_____

_____

Gratitude

_____

_____

_____

_____

Date: ___/____/_____   **Empathy Scale:**

Self-Care:

_____

_____

_____

Boundaries

_____

_____

_____

Gratitude

_____

_____

_____

_____

Date: ___/___/_____   **Empathy Scale:**

Self-Care:

_____

_____

_____

Boundaries

_____

_____

_____

Gratitude

_____

_____

_____

_____

Date: ___/___/_____   **Empathy Scale:**

Self-Care:

_____

_____

_____

Boundaries

_____

_____

_____

Gratitude

_____

_____

_____

_____

Date: ___/___/_____   **Empathy Scale:**

Self-Care:

_____

_____

_____

Boundaries

_____

_____

_____

Gratitude

_____

_____

_____

_____

Date: ___/___/_____   **Empathy Scale:**

Self-Care:

_____

_____

_____

Boundaries

_____

_____

_____

Gratitude

_____

_____

_____

_____

Date: ___/____/_____   **Empathy Scale:**

Self-Care:

_____

_____

_____

Boundaries

_____

_____

_____

Gratitude

_____

_____

_____

_____

Date: ___/____/_____   **Empathy Scale:**

Self-Care:

_____

_____

_____

Boundaries

_____

_____

Gratitude

_____

_____

_____

_____

Date: ___/____/_____   **Empathy Scale:**

Self-Care:

_____

_____

_____

Boundaries

_____

_____

_____

Gratitude

_____

_____

_____

_____

Date: ___/____/_____   **Empathy Scale:**

Self-Care:

_____

_____

_____

Boundaries

_____

_____

_____

Gratitude

_____

_____

_____

_____

Date: ___/____/_____   **Empathy Scale:**

Self-Care:

_____

_____

_____

Boundaries

_____

_____

_____

Gratitude

_____

_____

_____

_____

Date: ___/____/_____   **Empathy Scale:**

Self-Care:

_____

_____

_____

Boundaries

_____

_____

_____

Gratitude

_____

_____

_____

_____

Date: ___/____/_____   **Empathy Scale:**

Self-Care:

_____

_____

_____

Boundaries

_____

_____

_____

Gratitude

_____

_____

_____

_____

Date: ___/____/_____   **Empathy Scale:**

Self-Care:

_____

_____

_____

Boundaries

_____

_____

_____

Gratitude

_____

_____

_____

_____

Date: ___/____/_____   **Empathy Scale:**

Self-Care:

_____

_____

_____

Boundaries

_____

_____

_____

Gratitude

_____

_____

_____

_____

Date: ___/____/_____   **Empathy Scale:**

Self-Care:

_____

_____

_____

Boundaries

_____

_____

_____

Gratitude

_____

_____

_____

Date: ___/____/_____   **Empathy Scale:**

Self-Care:

_____

_____

_____

Boundaries

_____

_____

_____

Gratitude

_____

_____

_____

_____

Date: ___/____/_____   **Empathy Scale:**

Self-Care:

_____

_____

_____

Boundaries

_____

_____

_____

Gratitude

_____

_____

_____

_____

Date: ___/____/_____   **Empathy Scale:**

Self-Care:

_____

_____

_____

Boundaries

_____

_____

_____

Gratitude

_____

_____

_____

_____

Date: ___/____/_____   **Empathy Scale:**

Self-Care:

_____

_____

_____

Boundaries

_____

_____

_____

Gratitude

_____

_____

_____

_____

Date: ___/____/_____   **Empathy Scale:**

Self-Care:

_____

_____

_____

Boundaries

_____

_____

_____

Gratitude

_____

_____

_____

_____

Date: ___/____/_____   **Empathy Scale:**

Self-Care:

_____

_____

_____

Boundaries

_____

_____

_____

Gratitude

_____

_____

_____

Date: ___/____/_____   **Empathy Scale:**

Self-Care:

_____

_____

_____

Boundaries

_____

_____

_____

Gratitude

_____

_____

_____

_____

Date: ___/____/_____   **Empathy Scale:**

Self-Care:

_____

_____

_____

Boundaries

_____

_____

_____

Gratitude

_____

_____

_____

_____

Date: ___/____/_____   **Empathy Scale:**

Self-Care:

_____

_____

_____

Boundaries

_____

_____

_____

Gratitude

_____

_____

_____

_____

Date: ___/____/_____   **Empathy Scale:**

Self-Care:

_____

_____

_____

Boundaries

_____

_____

_____

Gratitude

_____

_____

_____

_____

Date: ___/___/_____   **Empathy Scale:**

Self-Care:

_____

_____

_____

Boundaries

_____

_____

_____

Gratitude

_____

_____

_____

_____

Date: ___/___/_____   **Empathy Scale:**

Self-Care:

_____

_____

_____

Boundaries

_____

_____

Gratitude

_____

_____

_____

_____

Made in the USA
Middletown, DE
31 August 2022

72804892R00070